Hereward College

LEARNING RESOURCES
CENTRE

This report is one of six on the RNIB survey. The others in the series are:

1 Shaping the future: research methodology and survey population
2 The educational experiences of 5 to 16 year-old blind and partially sighted children and young people
3 The educational experiences of partially sighted young people aged 16 to 25
4 The social life and leisure activities of blind and partially sighted children and young people aged 5 to 25
5 The health and wellbeing of blind and partially sighted children and young people aged 5 to 25

All reports in the series are available in braille, audio tape and on disk. All orders and enquiries should be sent to RNIB Customer Services, PO Box 173, Peterborough PE2 6WS, UK.

Telephone: 0845-702 3153
Email: cservices@rnib.org.uk

COVER PICTURE: study for a mural by **Tom Hunter** aged 21, a partially sighted student at Queen Alexandra College, Birmingham.

© **Royal National Institute for the Blind**
224 Great Portland Street, London W1W 5AA

First published 2000

ISBN 1-858-78449-2

Shaping the future

The experiences of **blind and partially sighted** children and young people in the UK

SUMMARY REPORT

by Issy Cole-Hamilton and Dan Vale
Royal National Institute for the Blind

Contents

Shaping the future research team

The **Shaping the future** research and reporting was undertaken by the following people.

The research

Part 1: Five to sixteen year-old blind and partially sighted pupils with additional complex needs

Kate Crofts (née Masters): Research design, fieldwork, initial analysis and reporting; additional analysis and reporting by **Liz Clery** and **Issy Cole-Hamilton** with **Sue Keil.**

Part 2: Five to sixteen year-old blind and partially sighted pupils who access the curriculum within the expected range for their age

Anita Franklin: Research design, fieldwork, initial analysis and reporting; additional analysis and reporting by **Sue Keil.**

Part 3: Sixteen to twenty-five year-old blind and partially sighted students

Lee Smith: Research design, fieldwork, initial analysis and reporting; additional analysis and reporting by **Sharon Da Cunha, Sue Keil** and **Issy Cole-Hamilton.**

Project administration: Angela Thompson with **Jessica Lubbock**

Project management: Issy Cole-Hamilton and **Louise Clunies-Ross**

Summary report: written by **Issy Cole-Hamilton** and **Dan Vale**

Acknowledgements

RNIB would like to dedicate these reports to all the children, young people and parents who contributed in so many different ways to the **Shaping the future** project. We give them our warmest thanks.

We would like to thank the LEA Advisory Teachers, Specialist Co-ordinators in further and higher education, staff in a variety of special schools, RNIB Student Advisors and staff in RNIB regional offices and schools, without whose support and assistance this work would have been impossible.

Particular recognition must go to the original research team: Anita Franklin, Lee Smith, Kate Crofts (née Masters) and Angela Thompson.

For their invaluable advice and support, we would like to thank Louise Clunies-Ross and the members of the Advisory group: Marianna Buultjens, Anna Cannings, Nigel Charles, Joyce Chatterton, Fazilet Hadi, Liz Hills, Sue Holbrook, Annette Hope, Sue Johnson, Rita Kirkwood, Olga Miller, Kishor Patel, Pratima Patel, Stephen Porter, Pat Robertson, Richard Stowell and Professor Mike Tobin.

We are also grateful for the contributions of Dot Lawton and the Family Fund, Brenda Smith (RNIB Care Training Service) Ruth Sinclair (National Children's Bureau) and our editor, Hilary Todd.

Issy Cole-Hamilton and Dan Vale

November 2000

Executive summary

Introduction

Blind and partially sighted children and young people in the United Kingdom are entitled to enjoy the same rights and responsibilities and to make the same types of decision as their sighted peers. In this, RNIB's **Shaping the future** summary report, over 1,000 young people between the ages of five and twenty-five show that, for many, their chances of being able to do this in the 21st century are being limited by a number of barriers.

These barriers will only be broken down when we understand that blind and partially sighted children and young people are not one homogeneous group. Their needs and aspirations are not met and cannot be met solely by a specialised niche market of providers. They want to do the things everyone wants to do – at the same time, in the same places and with the same people. They want to watch television, play computer games, hang out with their friends, plan their careers and go out on a date. Generic services that are aimed at all children and young people must take visual impairment and additional disability issues into account from the very earliest stages in planning.

In order for blind and partially sighted children and young people to live a full and equal life they must have **choice** and a **voice**. True choice depends on having sufficient information, support, confidence, resources and range of options. A true voice depends on the responsiveness of the people and structures that make up the young person's environment. Those who have difficulty communicating or learning as a result of more complex needs also have the right to have their voices heard and their rights respected.

The evidence given to us by blind and partially sighted children and young people and their parents shows that for them to have the same opportunities for personal and social development as others, they must challenge not only their visual impairment but also society itself. The participants in this survey are saying that:

- information is often not available in a format they can read at the time they need it;
- fully inclusive provision is not always available in education and leisure;
- independence and mobility are badly affected by lack of mobility education, hazards in the street and transport that is difficult to use;
- the attitudes and low expectations of other people can undermine self-confidence and lead to lack of self-esteem in blind and partially sighted children and young people.

Key findings

During 1998 and 1999, RNIB asked over 1,000 blind and partially sighted five to twenty-five year-olds, or their parents, about their experiences, needs and aspirations. There are 22,000 blind and partially sighted children aged 16 and under in the UK and we chose our sample to be broadly representative of them. We asked them to identify changes that could be made to improve their lives generally. The data were gathered by questionnaire and focus group, and the respondents were grouped by age and by learning ability. More detailed explanation of the findings can be read in the separate **Shaping the future** research reports listed before the contents page.

The children and young people

The children and young people who took part in the survey did so because they had sight difficulties that were severe enough to affect their day to day lives. Just less than one third also had additional complex difficulties which affected their communication, learning and motor abilities.

Those who accessed the curriculum within the expected range for their age, either at school or in further and higher education, are described in these reports as 'of around average learning ability'. Almost one in five of this group had little or no useful vision, three in five had severely reduced vision, and just over one in five, while requiring some support, had relatively good vision. Of the children and young people with complex additional needs, over three in ten had little or no useful vision and almost seven in ten had some useful vision.

It can be difficult for non-specialists to understand what these degrees of sight impairment actually mean. Only a few blind children and young people see nothing at all. Most have some perception of light, which may, for example, enable a young person to make out large shapes in a good light. Young people with 'severely reduced vision' in fact cover a wide spectrum depending on the eye condition they have; there are around 80 different eye conditions and it is possible to have more than one. Such impairment, however, may mean that they cannot use print as a means of learning and may have a considerable challenge to understand and make effective use of their environment. Some can read large or even standard print but have severe problems getting around. Some have the opposite challenge – they cannot read print, but they may be able to navigate their environment reasonably well. Those whose vision is 'relatively good' nevertheless need support to read, often preferring large print, and they are typically vulnerable in unfamiliar environments. Some young people need good light to make best use of the sight they have, while others function best in low light. The point is that every child and young person with impaired sight is different and has unique challenges and needs.

Visual impairment is frequently one manifestation of more complex conditions and accompanied by other impairments or difficulties. Nearly four in ten of the school-age pupils and one in five students in further and higher education, of around average learning ability, had additional disabilities.

These included, in particular, physical disability and hearing loss.

Most of the children and young people with complex additional needs had multiply disabling conditions which affected their communication, learning, mobility or day to day living skills. For example, one in four of the school-age children had cerebral palsy. Many had very complex needs affecting their ability to be independent in a number of ways. Two thirds of these children were dependent on others for almost all of their needs – to communicate, move around, wash, dress and eat. These children and young people will need high levels of support for their entire lives, though with the right education and support they can often achieve a great deal.

Education

The **Shaping the future** survey included pupils and students from a range of educational settings. The vast majority of those of around average learning ability were in mainstream education but a significant proportion attended specialist education designated for those with impaired vision. The children and young people with additional complex needs were, however, more likely to attend special schools, not specifically resourced for those with impaired vision.

The evidence from the survey shows that support in many areas must improve if inclusive provision is to meet the needs of blind and partially sighted pupils and students as well as designated specialist education for those with impaired vision does. Access to course material, equipment, activities and resources is often inadequate in mainstream education, as the following examples show.

- One in three blind and partially sighted pupils in mainstream secondary schools did not always get their school test and exam papers in their preferred format.
- One in four secondary pupils in mainstream schools said they did

not usually get handouts in a format they preferred.

- One in five secondary pupils did not have the necessary specialist equipment to do their homework.
- One in three mainstream secondary pupils said they felt left out of some classroom activities because of their impaired vision.
- Two in five secondary school pupils of around average learning ability said that their sight had affected their choice of GCSE or Standard Grade subjects.
- Geography, science and physical education were found to be less accessible than other subjects.
- Half of the parents whose children had complex additional needs were not in touch with their local authority specialist visual impairment teaching service.
- Two in three parents of children with complex additional needs who felt their child needed an 'interpreter'[1] said there was never one available.
- One in three parents of children with complex additional needs said their child was left out of activities at school because of their disabilities.
- At university, half of the students did not usually get their materials in the right format.
- Five in six university students said that their coursework took them longer than their sighted friends.

Social and leisure activities

Blind and partially sighted children and young people are restricted in their opportunities for leisure activities by a lack of accessible pastimes.

- Three in four parents of children with complex additional needs said there were no suitable local play activities for their child to attend during holidays.

---

[1] Increasingly 'intervenors' are working with these children to help them develop their communication skills and to express their needs and ideas. In focus groups parents were aware of their child's need for this type of support but tended to use the word 'interpreter' rather than 'intervenor'. The questionnaire therefore used the word 'interpreter'.

- Almost half of school-age children and young people of around average learning ability had experienced problems at clubs because of their impaired sight, prompting two in five of them to stop attending.
- More than one in four said there were clubs and activities which they would have liked to take part in at school, but had not done so, of whom one in six said this was due to their sight difficulty.
- More than one in three 16-25 year-olds had experienced problems at clubs or societies.

Getting out and about

Blind and partially sighted children and young people are less likely than sighted peers to travel independently and confidently because of a lack of mobility education and the difficulties they encounter on the streets and in using public transport.

Of those of around average learning ability:

- fewer than three in ten pupils in mainstream schools had been given mobility and independence education;
- nine in ten primary-aged children and over eight in ten of those of secondary age encountered difficulties when out and about;
- the street environment caused problems for nine in ten primary and seven in ten secondary school children and young people;
- lack of self-confidence in travelling was an issue for six in ten primary and over one in three secondary school pupils;
- two in three 16-25 year-olds also experienced difficulties in travelling.

Attitudes and awareness

While the majority of children and young people feel confident, the attitudes of others can make many feel isolated.

Among the 11-25 year-olds of around average learning ability:

- more than four in five felt that most people were willing to help once they understood about their sight;

- more than two in five said that others did not believe that people with sight difficulties could cope on their own;
- over one in four said they had been bullied a lot;
- children and young people were just as likely to have been bullied in specialist schools as in mainstream.

Most parents of blind and partially sighted children with complex additional needs feel that, in general, other people are very helpful, but:

- four in ten said that other people made rude remarks about their child;
- two out of three said people whispered about them;
- nine out of ten said that people stared at them.

Health and wellbeing

Children with complex additional needs and their parents are not getting the support or information about social and health care that they need.

- Only half the children with complex additional needs had a social worker.
- Only one in four parents thought all the agencies worked well together.
- Over one in three parents said they had negative experiences of hospital visits.
- Three in five parents had difficulty in finding suitable toys for their child.
- Nearly three in five children had no access to free short breaks or respite care.

Issues for action

RNIB is calling for:

1. Equality of access to books and information with sighted peers in whatever format is preferred – large print, tape or braille.
2. Improved access to technological advances including, for example, information and communications technology and digital technology.
3. More activities, particularly during the school holidays, which are accessible to blind and partially sighted children and

young people with and without complex additional needs.

4. More and better mobility and independence education, from an early age, for all blind and partially sighted children and young people.

Action to promote and deliver change can take a number of forms including, for example, the piloting of innovative schemes, training of existing and new staff, identifying, promoting and disseminating exemplars of successful practice, and campaigning.

To underpin and support these activities we will be emphasising the need for:

- greater recognition of the potential and abilities of all blind and partially sighted children and young people;
- a greater voice for children and young people themselves;
- increased support and resources for inclusive education;
- increased access to inclusive mainstream facilities and activities;
- more opportunities to take part in

specialised activities for those with similar abilities and experiences;
- appropriate, timely support for parents and families;
- greater collaboration between agencies working with and for blind and partially sighted children and young people and their families;
- young blind and partially sighted people and their advocates organising campaigning activities themselves.

RNIB's recommendations

1. Attitudes and awareness

Blind and partially sighted children and young people say that attitudes towards disabled people must change fundamentally. RNIB recommends that:

- schools, colleges and universities with policies relating to pupils and students with special educational needs should set targets for staff training in disability equality and awareness, including awareness of disability legislation;
- local authorities should ensure that induction and in-service training

for frontline staff working in public services includes a disability equality component;

- blind and partially sighted pupils should be actively involved in the development and monitoring of school anti-bullying policies;
- citizenship education should include a strong component on inclusion and disability equality issues;
- careers services should proactively promote employment prospects to blind and partially sighted young people.

2. Education

Equality in education

At the time of writing, the proposed Disability Rights in Education legislation extends many of the provisions of the Disability Discrimination Act 1995 to children and young people in education. Full implementation of the legislation will be fundamental to its success. RNIB recommends that:

- schools, colleges and universities should ensure that all disabled children and young people know about and fully understand their rights under the legislation, including their right to redress;
- teacher training at basic and in-service level should incorporate detailed discussion of the implications of the legislation for the day-to-day work of all education professionals;
- local education advisory teaching services should receive training in the implications of Disability Rights in Education legislation;
- education authorities should be required to make clear statements about how they will monitor the implementation of the Disability Rights in Education legislation.

Inclusive education

In the drive towards inclusive education, legislators and education providers must accept that inclusion is as much about the ethos and social life of schools, colleges and universities as it is about access to the curriculum. RNIB recommends that:

- the Government should ensure, through clearly defined and

monitored Quality Standards, that, as part of their inclusive education strategies, all mainstream provision is required to meet the needs of pupils with a range of sensory, physical and learning abilities and that this is properly resourced;

- all educational establishments' policies, practices and procedures should show how they will develop and monitor activities in which blind and partially sighted children and students are able to participate;
- the role of specialist provision for those with visual impairment in developing and supporting good practice in inclusive education should be fully evaluated;
- alterations to premises paid for through statutory funding schemes should always take account of the needs of blind and partially sighted pupils and students;
- Early Years and Childcare Partnerships throughout the UK should make the development of inclusive childcare and

out-of-school provision central to the planning of local services.

Accessible information

Children and young people should always have study and test material in a format they can use. RNIB recommends that:

- education establishments should have explicit policies to ensure that written information available to sighted pupils and students is always available to those who are blind or partially sighted, in their preferred format, at the time they need it;
- teachers should be given appropriate resources and time to allow them to plan for the provision of materials in the right format;
- education establishments should ensure that all materials produced comply with RNIB's guidelines for print, tape and braille (RNIB, 1999).

3. Social and leisure activities

Physical and social activities and opportunities to form friendships are crucial to the healthy development of any young person, but many blind and partially sighted children and young people feel excluded from these pursuits. RNIB recommends that:

- information about leisure activities should be made fully accessible and comprehensively publicised;
- staff involved in running leisure centres and organised activities for children and young people should be trained and supported to develop activities in which everyone can participate;
- more activities and equipment specifically designed for blind and partially sighted children and young people should be provided by education establishments and local authorities;
- local authorities should work with parents and young disabled people to design fully accessible play spaces;
- digital television and broadcasting should be made fully accessible to blind and partially sighted children and young people.

4. Getting out and about

The ability to negotiate public transport and the street environment safely and confidently is crucial to independence and self-confidence. RNIB recommends that:

- local authorities should ensure that mobility and independence education is available to all blind and partially sighted children and young people. These programmes should take place in domestic and new environments as well as in educational settings;
- transport operators should ensure that all journey and announcement information is fully accessible;
- all front line transport staff should receive disability equality and awareness training;
- help for blind and partially sighted children and young people and their carers should be available at all railway and coach stations at all times;
- public transport stations and vehicles should be fully accessible;
- local authorities should require clear and accessible signposting of

any hazards placed on pavements, that all crossings are accessibly marked and that vehicles and bicycles are kept off pavements;
· local authorities should include visual impairment criteria in their local transport plans.

5. Health and wellbeing

Comprehensive packages of care that are developed in collaboration with all relevant service providers, the parents and the child are crucial for the healthy development of all blind and partially sighted children. RNIB recommends that:

· social services and social work inspectors should carefully monitor assessment of children in need under the Children Acts and Order to ensure they promote equitable service provision;
· local authorities should ensure that there is adequate provision of a range of short break and respite services to meet the needs of different families;
· further resources should be put into the development of link worker and other similar schemes to improve inter-agency collaboration;
· Primary Health Care Trusts and other National Health Service providers should explicitly define how health services for children with complex needs can deliver the best possible care in collaboration with other services;
· health and benefits information should always be available and publicised in large print, tape and braille;
· information about eye conditions and local support networks should always be provided by health care professionals at the point of diagnosis.

Conclusion

The **Shaping the future** questionnaire surveys and focus groups provided us with unparalleled information about the current picture of life for blind and partially sighted children and young people in the UK. It is the first project that elicits a significant quantity of its evidence from the children and young people themselves in such depth. This provides RNIB with a firm mandate for encouraging the continuation of current good practice in service provision and urging change, where change is necessary.

Reference

RNIB (1999). **See it Right guidelines**. RNIB, London

Chapter 1

Part of a set of tiles designed by **Katie Nicholson**, a partially sighted 'A' level student at RNIB New College, Worcester.

Shaping the present

The Royal National Institute for the Blind (RNIB) believes that there are 22,000 children and young people aged 16 and under in the UK whose sight is impaired in such a way that they require additional support for their learning or mobility (Clunies-Ross, Franklin and Keil, 1999). Many of these children and young people have complex additional needs that affect their development and independence in a profound way. Drawing on a new RNIB survey, this report seeks to highlight the issues that they or their advocates say are important in their everyday lives.

This chapter puts the new survey in context. We start by looking at the findings of previous research into blind and partially sighted young people. We next explain the methodologies used in this research. The chapter then gives an overview of the political, legal and policy context which currently shapes the way visual impairment and the needs of children and young people are considered.

1.1 Previous findings

The first and only previous national survey of blind and partially sighted children and young people in the United Kingdom was undertaken in 1988 by RNIB (Walker et al, 1992). This survey revealed that more than half of all blind and partially sighted children and young people had another impairment, many having a multiplicity of disabilities which complicated their, and their families', needs. It also showed that many families did not receive the information and support they felt they needed. The survey, conducted in 1988, involved interviews with parents of 285 children.

When designing the current survey, we imagined that children and young people with visual impairment would often have the same views and experiences as their fully sighted peers. To check this assumption, we looked at a number of other recent surveys and made adaptations to some of their questions. These included the '2020 vision' survey (Industrial Society, 1997), 'Young people's social attitudes survey' (Roberts et al, 1996) and the 'Young people in 1994' study (Balding, 1995).

1.2 Methodology

For this survey, we decided to ask the young people themselves. During 1998 and 1999, three researchers asked over 1,000 blind and partially sighted five to twenty-five year-olds, or in some cases their parents, about their experiences, needs and aspirations. We also asked them to identify changes that could be made to improve their lives generally. The respondents were grouped by age and by learning ability. Approximately 130 children, young people and parents took part in focus groups to identify the themes for the questionnaire survey.

The main **Shaping the future** findings are based on questionnaire responses relating to 890 blind and partially sighted children and young people from local authorities and universities selected at random but ensuring representation from each geographical region. Of these:

- 220 were five to sixteen year-olds with additional complex needs;
- 425 were five to sixteen year-olds who accessed the curriculum within the expected range for their age;
- 202 were sixteen to twenty-five year-olds who accessed the curriculum within the expected range for their age attending school, sixth form colleges, colleges of further education and universities;
- 43 were sixteen to twenty-five year-olds with additional complex needs who were still in education.

Young people of 11 to 25 years old, who accessed the curriculum within the expected range for their age, described in these reports as 'of around average learning ability' responded to the questionnaires themselves. The views of the remainder of the children and young people were represented by their parents.

All the participants of around average learning ability were contacted via their specialist teaching or support services, and those with additional learning difficulties were also contacted via the Family Fund database and special schools. The Family Fund is an organisation which gives grants to families with disabled children and has a database containing information on over 60 per cent of the UK's most severely disabled children and young people.

The methodology used for the **Shaping the future** survey had a number of strengths. By employing a combination of focus groups and questionnaire research, findings could be verified and quantified. The consistency in findings of these two research techniques added strength to the findings. The decision to ask young people for their own views of their lives and the services they received also added credibility to the findings relating to their self image and personal experiences. The slight variation in methodologies and questions for the main survey also ensured that appropriate questions and research techniques were used for each group of students and pupils.

The response rates to the surveys varied from approximately 20 per cent to 40 per cent. So, although we were confident that we had a good cross section of the population, we cannot say that those who took part are truly representative of all blind or partially sighted children and young people in the UK today. We did, however, find that some groups of pupils and students, for example those in different types of school or college, or with different degrees of visual ability, had different experiences and views. Where this was the case we have reported the findings of these groups separately. One result of this is that some groups are small, making it unrealistic to extrapolate to the whole population. Nevertheless, where there is an indication that one group fared better or worse than another, this has been noted and provisos given.

The slightly different methodologies used for the different parts of the study do not always permit direct comparisons between the main groups of pupils and students. We have only made these comparisons when the question asked and the methodology employed have been the same. Where there are differences in the methodology, findings have been reported side by side and provisos given.

Of the children and young people represented in the survey, 40 per cent were girls and young women and 60 per cent boys and young men. This reflects the proportion found in other surveys which show that visual impairment and disability are more common among boys than girls.

We learned from an earlier profiling exercise that approximately 10 per cent of pupils and students supported by specialist education staff were from minority black and other ethnic communities. Only four per cent of those who chose to take part in our questionnaire survey of five to sixteen year-olds were from these groups. We do not know why they were under-represented but this is not uncommon in survey work. Among the 16 – 25 year old students, 12 per cent were from black and minority ethnic communities. The largest minority group in the survey were those who identified themselves as Pakistani.

Children and young people in the survey came from both urban and rural areas. The proportion of those from families who owned their own homes was similar to the rest of the population. However, the usual main income earner in the families was considerably less likely to be in employment than among the general population. Nearly 70 per cent of parents of children with complex additional needs had changed their patterns of work to care for their disabled child.

1.3 The policy context

1.3.1 Children's rights

The UK Government ratified the UN Convention on the Rights of the Child in 1991 and is responsible for ensuring that the rights of all children are promoted and protected. The Convention confers on children the rights to active participation both in their own lives and in society; to protection from harm and abuse; to the best possible health and health care; and to an education which enables them to develop to their full potential. It also gives them the rights to accessible information; to leisure and play opportunities; to an adequate standard of living; and to live wherever possible with their families. The Human Rights Act (1999) also enshrines the rights of children, young people and their families to privacy and to family life.

Articles 12 and 13 of the UN Convention confer on children the right to express their views in the manner of their choice and to have these views taken into account when decisions affecting them are taken. In all decisions that affect children, their best interests must be one of the primary considerations. In addition, disabled children have the right to the support and services which enable them to benefit from these rights, and their parents should be given the support necessary for them to protect and promote the rights of their child.

1.3.2 Perspectives on disability

There are as many different perspectives on the meaning of disability as there are individual experiences. There has been an increasing debate in recent years about the concept of disability and the prevailing view can have a major impact on the way in which services are developed and resourced.

In the past, blind and partially sighted people's difficulties in taking an active and equal part in society were generally attributed to the individual's impaired vision.

Solutions tended to focus on ways in which the impact of the person's visual difficulty or medical condition could be reduced, and resources were channelled into addressing the individual needs of each person.

In recent years, some disabled people have developed the 'social model' of disability. Their view is that the disadvantages they experience are a result of barriers created by society, not by their own impairments. One group of young people described the causes of their being disabled in the following way:

' . . . it is not this impairment which makes us a disabled person, it is society which makes us disabled. Society does not let us join in properly – information is not in accessible formats, there are steps into buildings, people's attitudes towards us are negative. So society puts barriers before us which stop us from taking part in society properly – it disables us.'
(Greater Manchester Coalition for Disabled People, reported in Morris, 1998)

Other disabled people feel that their experiences are the result of undeniable medical conditions, the recognition of which is an essential part of their identity and which determine their needs for very specific types of support.

Policy development today is informed by both these views. Disability Rights legislation aims to dismantle existing barriers to the full participation of disabled people in society. The law demands that all areas of society examine the way in which they provide goods, services and support and take all reasonable steps to ensure they are not discriminating against disabled people. At the same time health, welfare and education services are expected to ensure that, where a person has specific needs that cannot be met by adjustments to mainstream provision, these are properly assessed and addressed.

1.3.3 Inclusion

In recent years, throughout the UK, a number of welcome moves have been designed to address some of these societal barriers and to ensure appropriate specialist support is available. The most significant of these are:

- the Disability Discrimination Act 1995;
- impending Disability Rights in Education legislation;
- guidance relating to pupils with special educational needs;
- Early Years and Childcare Strategy planning guidance;
- initiatives in lifelong learning;
- proposals to reduce the social exclusion of young disadvantaged people, and;
- the establishment of the Disability Rights Commission (DRC).

1.3.4 The Disability Discrimination Act 1995

The Disability Discrimination Act (DDA) recognises that discrimination towards disabled people is widespread. It seeks to reduce such discrimination and the general lack of awareness of disabilities and disabled people. It also seeks to enshrine in law the rights of all disabled people to participate fully in an inclusive society.

In December 1996, the basic provisions of the DDA came into force. This made it unlawful to discriminate against disabled people either in employment or in their access to goods, facilities and services. There was little or no provision relating to education, and transport was covered separately by regulations governing new-build vehicles and the accessibility of licensed taxis.

In October 1999, provisions came into force requiring organisations providing goods and services to make 'reasonable adjustments' to ensure that disabled people could use their services. These adjustments included making changes to policies, practices and procedures, such as no-dogs policies, for guide dog owners, and providing auxiliary aids and services, such as assistance at stations and information in alternative formats. Providers were required to make alternative provision of the service where a physical feature made it difficult to use that service.

By 2004, service providers will need to have taken steps to remove, alter or provide means of avoiding physical features that make it impossible or unreasonably difficult to use a service. Service providers, including those involved in education services, should be phasing in improvements now to ensure compliance with the DDA.

1.3.5 Early years and childcare

Over the last two years the Government has been encouraging the development of early years and out of school childcare. Guidance on the Sure Start programmes, Early Excellence Centres and Early Years and Childcare Strategies encourages local authorities throughout the UK to develop inclusive provision in which disabled children are provided for with their non-disabled peers, both as very young children and in after-school and holiday play and care facilities.

1.3.6 Education

Since the Warnock report (1978), the 1981 Education Act in England and Wales, the 1981 Education (Scotland) Act in Scotland and the 1996 Education (Northern Ireland) Order in Northern Ireland, education policy in the UK has been to include children with special educational needs in mainstream education wherever possible. The policy of promoting inclusive education is central to the Disability Rights in Education legislation likely to be introduced in 2001.

The move towards inclusive education is reflected in the fact that, in the three decades since the Vernon report (1972) on the education of blind children in England, the number of designated specialist schools for those with impaired vision has dropped to less than half of its 1972 number, from 39 to 17. At present eight of these designated special schools for visually impaired pupils are maintained by local education authorities and nine by voluntary agencies, usually at their partial expense. LEA schools have tended to close at a quicker rate and there is no sign of this changing. These designated specialist schools tend to be clustered, with five out of the seventeen schools in the West Midlands and none in the north east of England. Increasingly these specialised schools are attended by pupils with more complex needs. At present there are three specialist schools for pupils with impaired vision in Scotland, one in Northern Ireland and none in Wales. The further and higher education systems have also become increasingly inclusive and all colleges and universities are expected to offer educational opportunities to disabled young people.

The growing recognition of the importance of parental involvement and partnership has worked both for and against inclusion. The arguments in favour of designated special schools for visually impaired pupils are usually based on their exclusive access to specialised facilities, equipment and staff expertise, a favourable pupil teacher ratio, extended day and holiday provision, and the benefits of mixing with other disabled children. The arguments against designated special schools focus on isolation from family, community and sighted peers, and a failure to prepare for life in an inclusive society.

Properly supported mainstream provision can currently provide for the special requirements of the vast majority of blind and partially sighted pupils and students. For those with complex additional needs that mainstream education is not yet designed to accommodate, there is a move towards expanding links to the mainstream system to support the inclusion process.

Regardless of mainstream/specialist arguments, there remains a significant challenge to make all types of education establishments more accessible for blind or partially sighted young people. The most frequently ignored policy in the inclusion debate is that of involving children and young people themselves in the planning process.

1.3.7 Lifelong learning

The current Government has signalled its determination to promote access to lifelong learning in the 'Learning to Succeed' White Paper (Department for Education and Employment, 1999) and similar documents in Scotland. The ethos behind lifelong learning is that education and training needs to be flexible in its mode of delivery, backed by clear information and advice, and supported by state, employers and individuals. In the White Paper the Government acknowledges that much needs to be done to make contact with and respond to the needs of learners and potential learners and that the current system is failing a significant section of the community, especially those who are the most vulnerable and disadvantaged.

1.3.8 Health and welfare

The Children Act (1989), the Children (Scotland) Act 1995 and the Children (Northern Ireland) Order 1995 define disabled children as being 'in need' and require that their support needs are assessed and provided for. The Department of Health has developed a new assessment framework for children in need in England and Wales which includes guidelines to assess the needs of disabled children and their families (Department of Health et al, 2000). Requirements for assessments are to be further strengthened under the proposed Disabled Children and Carers legislation. Health service proposals include the strengthening of the role of Primary Health Care Trusts in the commissioning and provision of local health services. It is unclear at present how community paediatric services will be affected by these changes.

1.3.9 Transport

The Department for the Environment, Transport and the

Regions has asked local authorities to draft Local Transport Plans or Strategies which set out their policies and plans for local transport over a five year period. These plans are to consider all types of transport and deliver five key objectives relating to the environment, safety, the economy, accessibility and integration.

RNIB has been campaigning intensively to have visual impairment criteria incorporated into every section of Local Transport Plans and Strategies. RNIB is also working with a number of different transport operators to ensure that vehicles are as accessible as possible, that all journey information is in accessible formats and that transport frontline staff are fully trained in disability issues.

References

Balding, J (1995). **Young people in 1994**. University of Exeter, Exeter

The Children Act 1989. HMSO, London

The Children (Northern Ireland) Order 1995. Northern Ireland Office, Belfast

The Children (Scotland) Act 1995. Scottish Office, Edinburgh

Clunies-Ross L, Franklin A, and Keil S (1999) **Blind and partially sighted children in Britain: their incidence and needs at a time of change**. RNIB for the Nuffield Foundation.

Department for Education and Employment (1999). **Early Years Development and Childcare Partnership Planning Guidance 2000 – 2001**. DfEE, London (Similar guidance exists in Scotland, Wales and Northern Ireland)

Department for Education and Employment (1999). **Learning to succeed: a new framework for post-16 learning**. Stationery Office, London

Department of Education and Science (1981). **Education Act 1981**. HMSO, London

Department of Health (2000). **Assessing children in need and their** families: practice guidance. Stationery Office, London

Department of Health, Department for Education and Employment and the Home Office (2000). Framework for the assessment of children in need and their families. Stationery Office, London

Disability Discrimination Act (1995). Stationery Office, London

Education and Industry Department (1981), Education (Scotland) Act, amending the Education (Scotland) Act 1980, Scottish Office, Edinburgh

Industrial Society (1997). 2020 vision survey. Industrial Society, London

Morris, J (1998). Accessing human rights: disabled children and the Children Act. Barnardos, Barkingside, p13.

Northern Ireland Office (1996). The education (Northern Ireland) order. SI no. 274. HMSO, Belfast

Roberts, H and Sachdev, D (1996). Young people's social attitudes survey. Barnardos, Barkingside

Vernon Report (1972) Department of Education and Science, The education of the visually handicapped. HMSO, London

United Nations (1989). UN Convention on the rights of the child. United Nations, Geneva

Walker, E, Tobin, M and McKennell, A (1992). Blind and partially sighted children in Britain: the RNIB survey. HMSO, London

Warnock Report (1978). Special educational needs: Report of the Committee of Inquiry into education of handicapped children and young people. HMSO, London

Chapter 2

Face made by **Jenny Rubine** aged 18,
a blind student at Queen Alexandra College, Birmingham.

Attitudes and awareness

'Educate the ones around you. Knowledge will help them empower you.'
Members of a **Shaping the future** focus group

'If parents are encouraged to project positive messages to the child, and not to be too over-protective (no matter how difficult this sometimes is), then we will see a new generation of independent and well-motivated young people who are able to take their place in society whatever their visual acuity.'
Parent of a five year-old girl

The participants in our focus groups, both young people and parents, ranked the attitudes of others as being one of the most important factors in their quality of life. This view was strongly reinforced in the questionnaire survey. When our respondents were asked to identify changes that might improve the lives of children and young people with sight difficulties in the future, a change in the attitudes of others came high on the list.

- Among the parents of primary school children of around average learning ability, nearly half put a change in the attitudes of others as one of their top three choices. One in five said it was the most important thing which should be changed.
- Of the five to sixteen year-olds of around average ability, nearly half put it in their top three and one in six as the most important factor.
- One in three sixteen to twenty-five year-olds put it in their top three.
- Three in every four parents of children with additional complex needs put it in their top three.
- Two in three parents of students with additional complex needs put it in their top three.

Those respondents who had more self-confidence and whose answers were in general more positive tended to have a happier experience of the behaviour of the general public, peers and professionals.

'In my opinion everyone's attitude to blindness is paramount. Resources and funding can only do

so much, but if people care and try, most difficulties can be overcome.'
Parent of a six year-old girl

'It would be helpful if more people are aware of the difficulties and troubles visually impaired people have to face in day to day life.'
12 year-old girl

Many focus group participants said that raising public awareness would aid disabled children's access to activities, independence and education. Parents also said that if the public were more aware of their child's needs, life would be easier for parents and siblings as well as the child.

'When K lost her eye . . . she spent the whole of reception term being bullied – school couldn't seem to prevent it. In Year 1 she chose to take her collection of artificial eyes into school. She let the children look and feel them, and told the children in her own words how her natural eye was making her very ill . . . The bullying stopped after this.'
Parent of a six year-old girl

The children and young people in the survey did not like to be perceived as different, and often avoided drawing attention to their sight difficulties by, for example, refusing to use low vision aids. Some parents of primary school children reported that their children felt uncomfortable about the eye condition itself.

• Over two in five secondary pupils said that they sometimes avoided doing things at school that drew attention to their sight difficulties.
• One in three parents said their primary school children sometimes avoided doing things at school that drew attention to their sight difficulties.
• Nearly one in two university students sometimes avoided doing things which drew attention to their sight difficulties.

'L hates her eye problems and lies and tells people she wears glasses because she has asthma.'
Parent of a six year-old girl

2.1 The awareness of professionals

The participants generally felt confident about the staff who worked with and supported them. For example nearly nine out of ten secondary pupils said they had someone to talk to if they had a problem at school.

A number of parents expressed concern that teachers did not fully appreciate the extent of their child's visual impairment. Children were sometimes labelled 'lazy' or 'slow learners' when the problem was, in fact, that extra time or appropriate equipment was needed.

'I would like people to be more tolerant when J has trouble getting her words out or falls over invisible objects because of her balance. Just more tolerance from everyone would make her feel more confident.'
Parent of a seven year-old girl

Conversely, some parents felt that the labelling of their child as 'disabled' led to lower expectations of achievement, or to over-protective attitudes of school staff.

'I feel that there is an attitude of low expectation... My child although only five is quite bright, but I don't believe he will get the support and attention he really needs as the safety issue gets in the way of everything. He actually needs less care as it is interfering with his independence...after all he is like any other child in most ways.' Parent of a primary pupil

2.2 The awareness of society

Offers of help and sympathy from the general public were often reported with, for example, four in five parents of pupils with complex additional needs saying that people were very helpful some or most of the time. Unfortunately though the experience of a large number of blind and partially sighted children and young people, and their parents, was also that fear of and prejudice towards disabled people were still common.

'We live in a village where prejudice against people with disabilities is still rife . . . my child is suffering because of this. I hope the future for all children with disabilities is a very much brighter one.'

Parent of a 10 year-old boy

Parents of children with additional complex needs, when asked about the reactions of others, said that, at different times and on different occasions, people stared at them, whispered about them, ignored them or overwhelmed them with well intentioned help:

- nine in ten said that some people stared at them;
- eight in ten said that other people looked away and avoided eye contact;
- seven in ten said that people whispered about them;
- five in ten said that some people made rude remarks;
- four in ten said that people often rushed in to help without asking whether help was needed.

Among children and young people of around average learning ability:

- over four in five said that most people were willing to help once they understood about sight difficulties;
- more than half said that most people thought all young people with impaired sight were the same;
- two in five said that most people did not believe blind and partially sighted children and young people could cope on their own;
- one in three said that most people talked about them as if they were not there.

2.3 The awareness of peers

Most children and young people of around average learning ability reported that they had friends and confidantes of their own age. That said, the evidence reveals experience of ignorance and exclusion.

'I would like fully sighted people to approach me more as because of my sight difficulties they often think I want to be left alone.'

21 year-old man

Often the attitudinal issue seems to hinge on a lack of awareness of what it means to have partial sight:

'I didn't recognise people, so they thought I was just rude.'
17 year-old girl

In other cases name-calling was reported as the most hurtful aspect:

'I am getting bullied at school because of my eyes. They called me "cockeye" and I'm scared of it because it's not fair on all the people who are like me with disabilities.'
Secondary school pupil

2.4 Taunting and bullying

The most worrying manifestations of prejudice were taunting and bullying.

'My daughter K . . . gets upset when people stare at her and call her names like "cat eye".'
Parent of a six year-old girl

- Half of the parents of primary school children believed their child had been bullied.
- Nearly three in five secondary pupils and students in further and higher education said that they had been bullied at some time.
- Bullying occurred to a similar extent in mainstream and all types of special schools and more often in sixth forms than in further and higher education.

Other research into the experience of bullying in the lives of children and young people with special needs found that this group were twice as likely to report being bullied as the control group (Nabuzoka and Smith, 1993, Whitney et al, 1994). Bullying can lead to major problems for the child or young person, including loss of confidence and self-esteem, as well as psychosomatic symptoms, and – in the most severe cases – depression or psychological problems (Kidscape, 1998). These problems may be shown in a number of ways such as not wanting to go to school, social withdrawal, or behavioural problems. The following comments by parents demonstrate some concerns:

'I helped my son fill in his questionnaire. The questions about bullying made him cry and he got very upset. It still hurts him so much.'

'The fact is with the bullying still going on he is now beginning to make excuses not to want to go to school.'

As one parent of a primary-aged child observed:

'Bullying for visually impaired children carries the added nightmare of the victim's being unable to identify his tormentors so that it is far harder for school to eradicate.'

Dawkins (1996) studied children and young people with conditions affecting their physical appearance, and identified four factors that could predict whether a child might be bullied. These were: being alone at break, being male, having fewer than two good friends in their class, and most importantly, receiving extra help in school. Many visually impaired children in our sample had one or more of these factors, thus increasing their chances of being bullied.

2.5 Self-perception

The building of confidence and self-esteem are central to helping a child combat isolation or bullying. Many of the children and young people taking part in the **Shaping the future** survey were positive and articulate. Those of around average learning ability were similar in many respects to other young people taking part in a major survey conducted by the National Society for the Prevention of Cruelty to Children (NSPCC) (Ghate and Daniels, 1997). For example, in both surveys:

- eight in ten saw themselves as cheerful;
- almost half said that they were popular at school;
- over half said they were confident.

However the young blind or partially sighted people in the **Shaping the future** study were more likely to say that they felt anxious, sometimes sad and sometimes lonely than those in the NSPCC survey. Of those in our survey:

- around one in three said they were anxious, compared with one in seven in the NSPCC study;
- nearly four in ten sometimes felt sad compared with three in ten in the NSPCC survey;
- nearly one in three sometimes felt lonely compared with one in ten in the NSPCC survey.

References

Dawkins, J L (1996). **Bullying, physical disability and the paediatric patient**. Developmental Medicine and Child Neurology, 38 (7), 603-612

Ghate, D and Daniels, A (1997). **Talking about my generation: a survey of 8 – 15 year olds growing up in the 1990s**. National Society for the Prevention of Cruelty to Children, London.

Kidscape (1998). **World first study into long term effects of bullying**. Press release, 21 April, London

Nabuzoka, D and Smith, PK (1993). **Sociometric status and social behaviour of children with and without learning difficulties**. Journal of Child Psychology and Psychiatry 34, 8, 1435-1448

Whitney, I, Smith, PK, and Thompson, P (1994). **Bullying and children with special educational needs**. In PK Smith and S Sharp (eds), School bullying: insights and perspectives. Routledge, London

Chapter 3

Figure by **Louise Simpson**, a blind student
at RNIB New College, Worcester.

Support in education

'If I can't read it I can't learn it.'
University student

This chapter is the longest of the summary report, reflecting the volume of questions relating either directly or indirectly to education. The evidence is presented in two different sections. The first is about those with complex additional needs and the second about those who access the curriculum within the expected range for their age.

3.1 Children and young people with additional complex needs

3.1.1 Type of school

Trends in educational provision for pupils who have special educational needs are constantly changing and have done so notably over the past 20 years. As a result of education legislation in the early 1980s, children and young people have increasingly been educated in mainstream schools and colleges and demand for some types of specialist provision has been decreasing.

However, of the 220 blind and partially sighted five to sixteen year-olds with additional complex needs represented in the **Shaping the future** study, only one in four attended mainstream schools. One in ten were being educated in special schools designated for those with visual impairment and the remainder in other types of special school. Those children and young people with the greatest needs for adult support were considerably more likely to attend special schools than those who were able to be more independent.

Of the 32 students with additional learning difficulties for whom information was available, 24 were in designated specialist provision for those with impaired vision, three were in mainstream provision and five were in other types of specialist provision. This group of young people is very small and we do not consider it reflects the situation for other students with complex needs in any way.

In the past disabled children often attended residential schools. Our study suggests that this is becoming much less common for blind and partially sighted children and young people who have additional complex needs. In 1988 RNIB found that 16 per cent of the children with additional complex needs were boarders (Walker et al, 1992) while among those represented in our survey, only six per cent stayed overnight at school. Of these, the children in specialist schools for those with visual impairment were more likely than others to be boarders.

3.1.2 Choosing a school and assessment of needs

Under current government policy, parents should be able to express a preference for the school their child attends. Of the parents of children with complex additional needs in our survey, fewer than half said they had been offered more than one school to choose from. The parents of those children and young people who were most dependent were least likely to feel they had been offered a choice of schools.

Most parents were happy to tell us what they considered to be the most important factors in choosing a school for their child. While these differed slightly depending on the type of school the child attended, the following priorities emerged:

- support for the child's visual needs;
- therapies available in the school;
- health support in the school;
- the fact that the school was near to the family home.

Both in focus groups and in written comments on the questionnaires, some parents described how they had had to fight with Education Authorities and Boards for appropriate school placements and Statements or Records of need. For example, one parent said:

'Expensive options are hidden by the LEAs because they don't want to pay for them. I had to find out about this place myself and then I really had to fight for the funding.'
Parent of a 14 year-old boy

If existing provision does not meet the child's needs, current legislation requires that a formal assessment is carried out and a Statement or Record is drawn up in consultation with teachers, other professionals and the child's parents. Guidance states that the process should take no more than six months.

Almost all the children with complex needs in the survey had a Statement or Record of need but fewer than one in three had been through the process within the recommended six months. For one in five children, the process had taken four or more years.

Statements and Records of need are reviewed annually to assess the child's progress and plan for future development. Guidance recommends that the parents and the child be actively involved in these reviews. The parents of 97 per cent of children in the survey said there were regular annual meetings at which most parents, eight out of ten, felt they were listened to all or most of the time. Almost all the remainder said they were listened to some of the time.

3.1.3 Specialist advisory services

Most education authorities and boards provide specialist advisory services to support blind and partially sighted pupils. However, not all these services are able to provide support for all the children with additional complex needs in the area. Those parents who were in touch with their local specialist service for visually impaired children clearly found this of benefit.

'We have had to fight for all that M has in school and at home, so far even to get our wonderful teacher for the visually impaired to visit four times a term.'
Parent of a boy aged seven

'The specialist teachers for the visually impaired are excellent, they are always very supportive and caring.'
Parent of a six year-old boy

However only one in four of the parents contacted via the

Family Fund said they were currently in touch with their local authority specialist teaching service for visually impaired children. This group represented half the pupils with additional complex needs and indicates clearly that a significant number of blind and partially sighted children were not getting the valuable support of these services.

3.1.4 Experiences at school

'He loves computers and was getting on well at his old school ... he has a computer at his new school but no-one knows how to make the words bigger so he is losing interest.'

Parent of a 17 year-old boy

In order for children to meet their full potential in education, a range of services and support must be in place when the child arrives at the school. In earlier discussion groups, parents had talked about the sorts of things they felt were important. They felt that the child should be able to adapt easily to the new routine, and that there should be plenty of staff available. They also felt that their child should be able to access all of the school, that the equipment the child needed should be in place at the start, and that transport for both parents and child to and from the school should not be too difficult. Only one in four parents felt that all these conditions had applied when their child started in their current school. However:

- three quarters of parents felt their child had adapted easily to the new routine;
- three in five parents said that the equipment required had been present;
- two thirds of parents thought that their child was able to access all of the school;
- nine in ten parents felt there were plenty of staff at the school to meet their child's needs;
- eight in ten parents believed their child was happy at school;
- eight in ten parents felt the staff at the school understood the child's needs.

The ability for a child to undertake school work successfully also depends on the environment in which that child is learning. Two-thirds of the parents said there were factors which made learning more difficult for their child.

- Nearly half felt that their child's work was hampered because other pupils' needs were very different.
- Nearly one in three said that noisy pupils were disruptive.
- A small number of parents with children in mainstream and other types of special school felt their child's work suffered because the teachers did not understand the sensory or physical needs of their child.

A child's education should also help develop self-confidence and teach daily living skills. In the focus groups, parents had also indicated that a wide choice of after-school activities was important for the development of their child. Only one in three parents agreed that their child's school had given them all these things.

- Only one in ten parents felt the school offered a wide choice of after-school activities.
- Only two in three parents felt their child was learning daily living skills.
- Just over two in three said the school had helped give their child confidence.

On the whole, it was the parents of children in specialist schools for those with visual impairment who felt their children were getting the best support and services.

3.1.5 Equipment and therapy

Children with complex needs require specialised support and equipment to develop and reach their full potential, both in society and in their learning. Some of these support services involve highly trained people or expensive equipment, but many do not. However, only one in seven parents felt that the things they thought important were always available for the child in the school. For example:

- two thirds of parents who felt their child needed an 'interpreter' said

that there was never one available;
- one in three parents who felt their child needed a play therapist said there was never one available;
- almost one in three parents who felt their child needed a mobility instructor said there was never one available;
- nearly a third of parents of children in mainstream schools said their child never had access to a specially adapted toilet.

'In our county we have no hydrotherapy pools or proper sensory rooms. For a very disabled child these are essential not luxuries. M has so few ways of getting pleasure and these are two of them.'
Parent of a boy aged seven

'... with greater budget I am sure the shortcomings of therapy at school would be addressed. Fighting for equipment is exhausting.'
Parent of a boy aged five

3.1.6 Activities at school

If disabled children are to play a role in society, they should not be excluded from activities at school on the grounds of disability. However, one in three parents said that their child was unable to take part in some activities as a result of their disability. The most common activites were physical education, swimming, drama, dance and trips and outings from school.

Children in mainstream schools were significantly more likely to be left out of some physical activities than those in other schools. Those in specialist schools for visual impairment were usually included in all class activities.

We were interested to know how parents and young people identified the difficulties experienced in participating in physically active pursuits and how this related to different perspectives on disability (see section 1.3.2). Of the parents giving reasons why they felt their child did not take part, nearly nine out of ten said the child's impairment was the restrictive factor. Only five of the 65 parents giving reasons said their child's activities were curtailed as a result of inadequate provision, including restricted physical access to venues, inadequate resources and lack of suitable staff support.

3.1.7 Satisfaction with school

On the whole the parents were well satisfied with their child's school. However, one in twelve parents were not satisfied with the school their child attended. Parents who were in touch with the specialist teaching service for visually impaired children were slightly more likely to be satisfied with the school, as were those who felt they were listened to at meetings. The reasons parents gave for being satisfied with their child's school included:

- the quality of the staff;
- the feeling that this was the best school for their child;
- the general support for their child's needs;
- the opportunities the child had to develop;
- the child being happy at the school; and

- good home/school relationships.

Other positive aspects included support for the child's visual needs and appropriate resourcing, therapies and equipment.

Reasons parents gave for not being satisfied included:

- inadequate support for their child's general needs;
- inadequate support for their child's visual needs;
- lack of suitable equipment;
- lack of suitable therapies; and
- poor school/home relationships.

3.2 Children and young people who access the curriculum within the expected range for their age

3.2.1 Type and choice of school

'The thing I like most about her going to a mainstream school is that when we go shopping or swimming all the children talk to her. They all acknowledge her even though she doesn't know they are there . . . I am so proud that people know her.'
Parent of a 12 year-old girl

The majority of blind and partially sighted children and young people in primary and secondary education are now educated in mainstream schools, with a minority attending special schools for visual impairment. Pupils in mainstream schools may be either in their local school with individual support from the specialist peripatetic teaching service, or in a school within their authority that has a dedicated resource base for blind and partially sighted pupils. In this survey these schools are called 'resourced schools'. A resourced school has additional staff, equipment and materials to meet the needs of blind and partially sighted pupils. The children are usually educated alongside their sighted peers, although there may be some occasions when they are taught separately in the specialist base.

In the **Shaping the future** survey, of the pupils of around average learning ability:

- nearly nine in ten attended mainstream schools, one in five of whom were at schools with dedicated resource bases;
- nearly one in ten attended special schools designated for pupils with impaired vision
- five pupils (3%) attended other types of special school.

The children and young people in our study tended to stay in the same type of education provision throughout their compulsory schooling. Those who attended specialist provision at primary level were most likely to remain in specialist provision and those who began their schooling in mainstream schools tended to continue in mainstream education. Where pupils did move between types of school similar numbers moved from mainstream to specialist and from specialist to mainstream schools.

The proportion of pupils with no other disabilities attending residential school was small – only two per cent. This compared with eight per cent in 1988 when the previous RNIB study was conducted (Walker et al, 1992).

However, pupils attending designated specialist schools for those with impaired vision tended to have to travel long distances between school and home and a number of parents expressed concern over the distance that had to be travelled to the nearest appropriate school.

'My son is eight years old, he has no vision. I do not understand why there are so few schools for him to go to. We live 80 miles from London and he has to travel to London and back every day.'
Parent of an eight year-old boy

Others felt that local schools could provide a more than adequate schooling experience:

'Provided adequate and appropriate support is provided, young people with visual difficulties can thrive in their local schools.'
Parent of a girl aged five

Most pupils were in the appropriate academic year for their age.

Of the students of around average learning ability in sixth forms, sixth form colleges and colleges of further education:

• more than two in three were in mainstream education, one in ten of whom were in 6th forms in schools with resource bases;
• three in ten were in designated specialist provision for those with impaired vision;
• four students (three per cent) were at other types of specialist provision.

3.2.2 General feelings about school, college and university

The children and young people were generally happy at school, college or university and satisfied with the support they received. However, there were significant numbers who did not receive support at the time they needed it and who felt unhappy about their ability to participate in activities. A number were uncomfortable about bullying, being left out of activities with the rest of the class and not always being supported in the way they would have wished.

The pupils of secondary school age were asked to identify the three most important factors in making a good school. They gave the following answers:

- 81 per cent said 'a teacher who listens';
- 71 per cent said 'having enough help in the classroom';
- 52 per cent said 'having enough resources';
- 43 per cent said 'no bullying'.

All of the pupils at specialist schools designated for blind and partially sighted pupils agreed with the statement that they usually received the help they needed at school. This contrasts with the 14 per cent of mainstream and 10 per cent of resourced mainstream pupils who considered that they were not getting all the help they needed at school. Over half of the parents of primary age pupils and secondary pupils felt that visual difficulty sometimes made it hard to keep up during lessons.

Among sixth form and further education college students, 11 per cent said they did not usually get the help they needed, and this doubled for the university and higher education students, 23 per cent of whom said they did not usually get the help they needed.

3.2.3 Statements and Records of need

Pupils with special educational needs do not all have Statements or Records of need. If a school is able to provide adequate support for a pupil's needs without extra resources, a Statement or Record is not required. However a substantial number of pupils with a significant visual impairment were found to be progressing through the education system without a Statement or Record of needs.

- Only 71 per cent of pupils in the survey had a Statement or Record of needs.
- One in ten parents said they knew nothing about Statements or Records of needs.

In the earlier RNIB survey, we found only 63 per cent of pupils had been given a formal assessment of their special educational needs (Walker et al, 1992). Our results indicate that parents have greatly increased their awareness of formal educational assessment over the last 10 years, from around four in ten in 1988 to nine in ten today.

- On average it took between six months and one year for parents in our sample to obtain their child's first Statement or Record of needs.
- Eight per cent of pupils had to wait over two years before obtaining their Statement or Record of needs.

The Statement or Record was no guarantee of adequate support however. As one parent of a secondary pupil observed:

'It always sounds alright on paper, but at school, B's helper is often off sick or has to go to another child. She finds this a worry as she cannot see the board or read small print, she often gets behind with her work, but on paper they assure me she has her 15 hours a week help.'

All 37 sixth form college students had had their learning needs assessed at the start of their course, as did 80 per cent of further education college students. However, 37 per cent of university and higher education students had not had their learning needs assessed at the start of their course.

3.2.4 Reading

'We have an equal right to information – information improves quality of life.'
A focus group participant

'I think there should be more big print available, especially story books and there should be better leisure activities.'
Girl aged 12

'I did not get extra time. I had a lot of problems with lecturers. When I said I couldn't see the blackboard, they would write things bigger which didn't help. Course notes were in too small print. This was constant. They never learned.'
Young person in a focus group

Children and young people who are blind or partially sighted learn through a variety of media. Some read standard print, using low vision aids; some require large print; others read and write in braille using a range of technology to support their learning. Audio tape and computers are increasingly widely used.

It is not unusual for blind and partially sighted children and young people to use more than one medium for reading. For example, of the pupils in our study:

- 64 per cent liked large print;
- 35 per cent liked standard print;
- 18 per cent liked computer disk;
- 12 per cent liked tape;
- 10 per cent liked braille.

Of the post-16 age group:

- 59 per cent liked large print;
- 35 per cent liked standard print;
- 23 per cent liked computer disk;
- 19 per cent liked tape;
- 20 per cent liked braille.

Although 58 per cent of pupils used standard print, only 35 per cent expressed a preference for it.

- However, only 34 per cent used standard print exclusively.
- The remaining 24 per cent used combinations of media such as standard print and large print, or standard print, large print and disk.
- Amost all who liked standard print and who like braille used these reading media at school.
- Among those who liked large print, 85 per cent used it, often supplemented by other media.
- Only two out of three mainstream pupils usually got their school books in the format they required.
- Only three in four mainstream pupils usually got their class handouts in their preferred format.
- One in four of all secondary pupils experienced difficulties in using the school library.
- More than one in three secondary pupils and a quarter of parents of primary school children stated that they usually had to wait for handouts in the format they preferred.

It is worth noting here that in a study investigating the use of low vision aids by blind and partially sighted pupils in mainstream schools, researchers found that pupils admitted to using various strategies to avoid using such aids, which included requesting large print. Teachers sometimes refused to provide large print in order to encourage the use of low vision aids (Mason and Mason, 1998).

'Exams are often enlarged, but occasional class handouts are often small type and poorly reproduced. At home for study/research I often have to read for him because he loses his place and it takes too long. He is a bright, fairly academic pupil.'
Parent of a secondary school pupil

One in ten of all pupils of around average learning ability in the survey used braille. One in three of these children attended specialist schools for those with impaired vision where they all received braille lessons. Two in three attended mainstream or resourced mainstream schools where just over two in three said they received braille lessons. A high proportion of primary school children in mainstream schools were taught braille by specialist peripatetic teachers.

If anything, universities were felt to be even less adequately equipped to meet the needs of blind or partially sighted students than schools. Nearly half (47 per cent) of students in university and higher education did not usually get books in their preferred formats.

Of the sixth form and further education college students, those in the mainstream were less likely to get books in their preferred formats – 36 per cent did not usually receive books in their preferred formats, compared with 17 per cent of those in specialist further education colleges for blind or partially sighted students.

Clearly these findings have implications for how well blind and partially sighted children and young people achieve at school, college and university. Combined with the difficulties many encountered in using libraries, it is not surprising that many found that their work took longer than that of their sighted peers. Our findings indicate that it was children and young people in mainstream schools who were most disadvantaged by a lack of appropriate materials and support. Those in mainstream schools additionally resourced for blind or partially sighted pupils appeared to fare better, and pupils attending specialist schools for blind and partially sighted pupils were, as a group, better resourced and supported educationally than their mainstream counterparts.

3.2.5 Use of libraries

'Because I couldn't read the signs on the wall, I couldn't read which book was which, and once I'd found the book it was very difficult to see the page you want. It takes a very long time to find anything.'
Young person in a focus group

More than one in four secondary pupils at mainstream or resourced mainstream schools experienced difficulties in using the school library. This compared with only one of the 21 pupils who attended specialist schools for blind and partially sighted pupils.

Library use proved even more difficult at university, where it is arguably even more vital to course work. As many as 39 per cent of university or higher education students said they found it difficult to use the library, compared with 11 per cent of further education college students and 14 per cent of sixth formers. While only 12 per cent of university students reported not having used the library, showing its importance, 26 per cent of sixth form and 23 per cent of further education college students had not done so.

3.2.6 Access to the curriculum, examinations and homework

'I would have liked to have done the sciences but the experiments and close detailed

work would have been too much.'
Student in a focus group

'I do not take part in physical education because I sometimes can be a danger to myself or others because of my sight.'
Secondary school pupil

'I started to do computer science. The computer department did not have anything to enlarge the print so I didn't do well. So I dropped computer studies.'
Student in a focus group

We found that children and young people with impaired sight did not always have access to the full curriculum.

- Geography and science were the subjects that secondary aged pupils found the most challenging.
- Drama was the subject that presented pupils with the fewest difficulties.
- Young people at specialist schools for blind and partially sighted pupils were less likely to feel that their sight difficulty impaired their performance at school.
- One in ten pupils had difficulty

with particular subjects because of the teacher's use of the blackboard , whiteboard or overhead projector.
- One in three secondary pupils stated that their sight had influenced their choice of GCSE or Standard Grade subjects.

Among older students, 27 per cent of sixth form, 20 per cent of university and 16 per cent of further education college students felt their sight difficulties had affected their choice of subjects. The most commonly given reasons were practical problems and problems with intensive reading or use of print materials.

Tests and examinations could pose particular difficulties, typically because the papers were not always in the correct format.

- One in four of the pupils questioned did not always get test or answer papers in the right format.
- One in five pupils said that test or exam papers had not always arrived at school on time.
- Pupils in mainstream schools were

more likely to have difficulties in obtaining their test and answer papers in the correct format.

- Four out of five pupils were satisfied with levels of lighting and desk space in the exam room.
- Fifteen per cent of pupils did not usually find the lighting in exam rooms sufficient.
- Eighteen per cent of pupils did not have sufficient desk space in the exam room.
- One third of sixth form and university students had received late exam papers on at least one occasion, as had 11 per cent of further education college students. Mainstream students were more likely to get late papers.
- Nine out of ten further education college students always got exam papers in preferred formats compared with just over eight in ten sixth formers and university and higher education students.
- Around nine out of ten university and sixth form students got extra time for exams, as did eight out of ten further education college students.

Homework was another challenge. Over half of the pupils (57 per cent) questioned felt that it usually took them longer to do their homework than their sighted friends. While 41 per cent of further education and 46 per cent of sixth form students felt their homework/coursework took them longer than their friends, 83 per cent of university students thought this. Mainstream students were more likely to think this. Twenty one per cent of secondary pupils considered that they did not have the necessary equipment at home to do their homework/coursework, as did 16 per cent of post-16 students.

3.2.7 Equipment and aids

A quarter of secondary pupils and parents of primary school children felt that they did not have all the necessary equipment at school. Over half the cases of dissatisfaction with the pupil's Statement or Record of needs were due to a perceived lack of resource provision. A few pupils lacked quite basic equipment such as magnifiers, lamps/lights and braillers. However, many children and young people of all age groups were concerned about the stigma attached to using specialist equipment:

- 20 per cent of the pupils questioned stated that they disliked using some equipment; 14 per cent from the primary age group and 26 per cent of secondary pupils.

Access to information technology was however quite encouraging.

- Forty five per cent of all the pupils questioned had a personal computer at home.

- Thirty eight per cent of secondary pupils had access to the Internet.
- Ten per cent of primary pupils had access to the Internet.
- Ninety eight per cent of 16-25 year-old students used computers.

3.2.8 Activities

'B often gets left out on the playground as they play football and he finds playtime the hardest part of the day.'
Parent of a primary school child

More than a quarter of secondary pupils stated that they 'sometimes got left out of class activities because of their sight difficulties'. Twenty nine per cent of primary pupils were sometimes left out at break times and one in five sixth form and further education college students sometimes felt left out of social activities. One in four university students sometimes felt left out.

3.2.9 Careers advice

'I was told I could not do certain jobs when I could do – management, things like that. Generally I was told I could be a secretary.'

Young person in a focus group

- 96 per cent of post-16 students had received careers advice at some point.
- 88 per cent of those who had received advice had received it from a school careers adviser.
- 84 per cent were satisfied with the advice given.

Over a third of students had been told that they could not do a job they had been interested in because of their sight difficulties, including retail and office work. Only 20 per cent had been trained to find out about job vacancies and only half felt confident about finding out about job vacancies.

'They tend to steer me towards colleges and jobs just for the disabled. They never try to integrate me into society.'

Young person in a focus group

References

Mason, HL and Mason, BF (1998). **The use of low vision aids in mainstream schools by pupils with a visual impairment**. Report to the Viscount Nuffield Auxiliary Fund. Birmingham University, Birmingham.

Walker, E, Tobin, M and McKennell, A (1992). **Blind and partially sighted children in Britain: the RNIB survey**. HMSO, London.

Chapter 4

Picture by **Donna Hay** age 14, a partially sighted student at Linden Lodge School, London.

Social life, leisure and travel

4.1 Social life and friendships

Friendships form an important part of the social life of most children and young people and those in our study proved no exception. Among those of around average learning ability, almost all of the students over 16 years old and nine in ten secondary pupils said that friends were important to them. Parents of three in four primary school pupils said friends were important to their child and parents of nine in ten pupils with complex additional needs said their child showed pleasure in the company of other children while at home.

Friendship patterns among the children and young people of around average learning ability in our survey were similar in some ways to those in the NSPCC survey of nearly 1,000 children and young people aged 8 to 15 years, but there were some differences (Ghate and Daniels, 1997).

• One in three pupils and students in our sample wished they had more friends to talk to compared with one in ten in the NSPCC survey.

• One in three pupils in our survey said they sometimes felt left out by their friends compared with one in five in the NSPCC survey.

The older pupils and students were more likely to say that most of their friends also had sight difficulties. Those in specialist provision for pupils and students with visual impairment were also less likely to have a lot of friends where they lived. For example:

• among primary school children, parents of over half those at specialist schools for visually impaired pupils but only one in 75 at mainstream schools said most of their friends had sight difficulties;

• among those at secondary school, six in seven pupils at specialist schools for those with impaired vision but only one in twenty five in mainstream schools said most of their friends had sight difficulties;

• of those from 16 to 25 years old, over three in five of those in specialist provision designated for those with impaired vision, compared with just under two in five in mainstream provision and university said most of their friends had sight difficulties.

Friendship patterns among the children and young people with complex additional needs were different. Eight in ten parents said their child showed pleasure in the company of other children at school, nine in ten said their child showed pleasure in the company of other children at home and nearly four in ten said their child had a special friend.

4.2 Leisure activities

The evidence from this survey shows that, contrary to the stereotype, blind and partially sighted children and young people join in a wide range of pursuits. Unlike their sighted peers, however, their activities are often restricted because the pastime is inaccessible, or because they or others perceive that involvement would not be appropriate.

'Whilst my son copes well when joining in activities and enjoys doing so, I have not found any leisure centres or clubs that understand the needs of a child with sight problems. Steps are not painted and signs are not always printed in large clear print. In unfamiliar surroundings help is needed for a time to show the child around.'

Parent of a seven year-old boy

Watching TV or videos, listening to music and playing on computers were the most popular activities for school-aged pupils generally. The older students were more likely to spend their leisure time socialising with their friends.

- Over four in ten primary school children and one in three secondary pupils of around average learning ability said watching TV was one of their main leisure occupations.
- Three in ten children of both age groups spent much of their leisure time using computers or playing computer games.
- One in three children and young people with complex additional

needs liked to watch television and videos.

- Three in ten children and young people with complex additional needs liked listening to music.
- Over four in ten students aged 16-25 of around average learning ability spent their time socialising with their friends.

As television and interactive broadcasting are set to become predominantly digital media, it is clearly vital that digital information is designed to be accessible to blind and partially sighted young people. Voice-out technology, clear print on screen and good navigability are the key issues that will allow these young people to benefit fully from changes to broadcast media.

The most popular physical activity was swimming. One in five of all the groups listed swimming as one of their main out-of-school activities. Smaller numbers of children and young people enjoyed ball games, gymnastics and martial arts, skateboarding and cycling.

However many young people felt that these and other organised activities were not readily available to them.

- One in five young people had stopped going to clubs or other activities because of problems they had encountered there. This was frequently at organised clubs and groups.
- One in five children of average learning ability felt they were denied access to activities because of inadequate staff support, lack of access equipment or access difficulties.

Lack of support within the activity was often the reason given for not joining in:

'I'm not allowed to take ballet exams beyond a certain level. Can't see what the instructor is doing.'
18 year-old woman

'I can't get music put into braille easily.'
20 year-old woman

Sometimes the service was not prepared to support blind or partially sighted children:

'Where I live I feel that my son is treated very poorly . . . the leisure centre which has some very good activities available will not have special needs, I find it very sad.'

Parent of a 10 year-old boy

Other reasons given were embarrassment or the attitudes of other children:

'I don't want to make a fool of myself. I'd feel all embarrassed if I couldn't see what the teacher was doing in aerobics.'

20 year-old woman

'My son attends a boarding school for the blind and at weekends he is a recluse. There is nowhere for D, such as clubs or activity centres for his needs. He did join a local club but has left as the other children took the mickey out of him with his eyesight, and the children around where we live tease and torment him, so this is why my son does not go out.'

Parent of a 12 year-old boy

Some children and parents wanted activities to be available with other blind or partially sighted children:

'It would be nice if she could go places with other children of her own age and disability, where she could be safe and experience "normality" and do activities together where she wouldn't be "the one left sitting" because of her poor vision and mobility.'

Parent of a primary school pupil

For the young people aged 16 to 25 it was very important that they felt able to go out to clubs and pubs. Again the message was that they were not always being made welcome.

'We went there once but now no-one at the college is allowed in because they are considered a health hazard – dangerous to other people in case we walk into people or broke something. We were told to take our custom elsewhere.'

18 year-old woman

4.3 Children and young people with complex additional needs

For children with complex additional needs, provision of leisure and play opportunities is very inadequate. Over three in four parents said that there were not enough suitable opportunities for their children during school holidays and nearly six in ten said there were activities their child would have liked to take part in but found it difficult. These activities included swimming, ball games, socialising with friends, horse-riding and cycling.

A minority of parents cited social barriers to their child's participation in activities, including lack of suitable equipment, lack of appropriate adult support and lack of awareness among staff of the needs of the child. The majority, however, saw their child's disability as the main reason they could not take part in those activities. However, when asked specific questions, parents acknowledged a number of problems in finding suitable leisure opportunities for their children. For example:

- six in ten had difficulty finding suitable toys for their child;
- six in ten said that play areas did not have swings their child could use;
- half said there was no good local play scheme their child could attend;
- nearly half felt sports attendants did not help their child to have fun.

Parents identified funding as an important obstacle to their child's social life. They gave examples of instances where a need for specific equipment had been identified but funding had not been readily available from appropriate authorities.

'We don't get any funding for leisure equipment. We buy ordinary stuff and adapt it.'
Parent of a boy aged eight

4.4 Mobility and independence

A crucial element of being able to participate fully in activities is having the confidence to negotiate the street environment and public transport safely. For this to be possible there must be adequate mobility and independence education as well as streets that are well marked, free of hazards and well lit. The children and young people reported that this was not the case.

'Going places at night is difficult as it is much harder to find your way and you are more likely to have an accident or run into trouble.'
25 year-old man

It was even more difficult and potentially dangerous for younger children:

' . . . uneven surfaces and steps are drawbacks, N frequently falls down by not being able to see properly.'
Parent of 14 year-old girl

The survey revealed that, among those of around average learning ability, the vast majority of problems were environmental, with the street environment causing problems for many. Lack of self-confidence was also an issue for significant numbers of children and young people.

- Over nine in ten primary and over eight in ten secondary school children encountered difficulties when out and about.
- The street environment caused problems for nine in ten primary and seven in ten secondary school children.
- Lack of self-confidence in travelling was an issue for six in ten primary pupils, over one in three secondary school pupils and four in ten 16-25 year-olds.
- Two in three 16-25 year-olds also experienced difficulties with the environment.

'People are often unfriendly and don't get out of the way, it's hard for me to avoid crowds. Cyclists also cause problems for me as they ride on the pavement. Road works as well. Some crossings can be difficult to see the red or green man.'
21 year-old man

4.4.1 Specialist mobility lessons

Mobility skills are fundamental to the development of a visually impaired child or young person's independence and self-confidence. Yet mobility education remains a marginal element of the curriculum, which is not in the spirit of the Department for Education and Employment's stated commitment to fully inclusive education.

- Nearly two in three pupils attending specialist schools for blind and partially sighted pupils had received mobility education.
- Fewer than three in ten pupils in mainstream schools had received mobility education.
- Only three of the 117 pupils who had mobility education had this built into their timetables.
- One in twenty 16-25 year olds of around average learning ability had had no mobility education but would have liked it.

Mobility education took place mainly in the school or college environment and very few children and young people had been educated in other locations. For example:

- only one in fourteen pupils had received mobility education in their home area;
- only one in seven secondary school pupils had received mobility education in shopping centres and supermarkets.

References

Ghate,D and Daniels, A (1997). **Talking about my generation: a survey of 8 – 15 year-olds growing up in the 1990s.** National Society for the Prevention of Cruelty to Children, London.

Chapter 5

Figure by **Year 9 students** at
RNIB New College, Worcester.

Health and wellbeing

'Raising children with disability is a totally consuming way of life. It obviously changes your attitude to life and your behaviour – in some ways it brings out qualities you never dreamed you possessed.'
Parent of a seven year-old girl

Although most of the children and young people represented in the survey had visited their eye clinic during the past year, the vast majority enjoyed good general health. In fact:

- over half the pupils of around average learning ability were perceived by their parents to be in excellent health;
- one in five parents of pupils with complex additional needs perceived their child to be in excellent heath;
- nearly half of the older students perceived themselves to be in excellent health.

5.1 Levels of sight

A range of medical conditions had resulted in impaired vision for these young people and their visual ability varied widely. To assess the impact on the child or young person's vision, six levels of visual ability were developed for those of around average learning ability and two for those with complex additional needs. Among those of around average learning ability represented in the survey:

- eight per cent of school children and 15 per cent of older students were functionally blind with no light perception. They needed aids, equipment and accessible media in the classroom and orientation and mobility education;
- eight per cent of school age and 27 per cent of older students had light perception and very low vision. They required visual aids, equipment and accessible media in the classroom and some degree of orientation and mobility education;
- 32 per cent of school age and 16 per cent of older students had light perception but were unable to read standard newspaper print and had poor distance vision. Visual aids, equipment and accessible media were needed and these young

people could be vulnerable in unfamiliar environments;

- six per cent of school age and three per cent of older students were only able to read print with the use of visual aids, and needed equipment and accessible media in the classroom. They were able to be completely independent within the general environment;

- 22 per cent of school age and 20 per cent of older students had poor distance vision and while being able to read standard newspaper print were likely to require mobility education;

- 24 per cent of school age and 19 per cent of older students had relatively high levels of vision but still required support because of poor image quality, visual perceptual problems or other sight difficulties.

Of those with complex additional needs:

- 32 per cent had little or no useful vision;
- 68 per cent had some useful vision.

Childhood visual impairment is generally apparent in the early years. The earlier RNIB survey found that one in two children had their sight condition medically confirmed by their first birthday, and two out of three were diagnosed by the age of two (Walker et al, 1992). In the current survey, nine out of ten children of around average learning ability had their sight condition diagnosed before the age of five, and two out of three were diagnosed during their first year. Later diagnosis of visual impairment was not associated with any particular sight condition.

5.2 Medical conditions and additional impairments

Childhood visual impairment is frequently associated with conditions that affect the child's development in other ways. Of the children and young people in our study, of around average learning ability:

- three in ten of those of school age had additional impairments.

Almost four in ten of these had chronic medical conditions, just over two in ten had motor disorders, two in ten had physical difficulties, two in ten had learning difficulties and just over one in ten had impaired hearing;

- two in ten of the older students had additional impairments of whom just over three in ten had physical difficulties, three in ten had chronic medical conditions and three in ten had impaired hearing.

Many of these children and young people were affected in more than one way.

Most of the children and young people with complex additional needs also had difficulties with communication, mobility and their day-to-day care needs. Eight out of ten were highly dependent on others for all or part of their daily activity.

For example:

- four in ten were unable to communicate through speech;
- fewer than four in ten were able to move around independently without human assistance;
- five in ten required help with all basic care needs such as eating, drinking, washing, dressing and using the toilet;
- almost nine in ten exhibited some types of challenging behaviour with nearly three in ten often being violent and aggressive.

5.3 Use of health and social welfare services

Unsurprisingly, the children and young people in our survey were fairly regular users of health services, in particular those relating to eye health. During the previous year:

- nine in ten of school age pupils of around average learning ability had visited the eye health services;
- nearly three in four children and young people with complex additional needs had visited the eye health services.

Almost all the children and young people with complex additional needs had visited the health services during the previous year including in particular, family doctors and paediatricians, about health issues not related to the child's sight.

The families' experiences of the health services were not always positive and parents of those with complex additional needs frequently felt that they were not getting the level of support that they and their children needed.

For many, the experience of visiting hospitals had many negative aspects, for example:

- nearly four in ten parents said someone had to take time off work to go to the hospital;
- over one in four had a journey taking more than an hour to get to hospital;
- one in five said it cost 'a lot of money' to go to the hospital;
- one in three children did not like going to hospital.

There were also concerns about the quality of the consultation when they were at the hospital. While nearly three quarters of parents felt that seeing new doctors and hearing a new opinion was useful,

one in four found it confusing. Just over five in ten thought that health professionals seen for the first time had not read the child's notes and needed to spend a lot of time going over the child's history. Four in ten parents felt there were too many people to see.

'I am really concerned about my child's condition. I don't know where to get the information about her condition and about possible treatments.'
Parent in a focus group

'S has Downs Syndrome. I wasn't told to have his hearing and eyesight checked until he was four years old, now he is partially sighted and semi-deaf. I'm really fed up.'
Parent of a six year-old boy

The need for prompt and accurate information about eye and other health conditions was mentioned by many of the parents questioned.

'... for new parents of children with disabilities help and information is still not freely offered and it can take many years before they receive everything available to them and their child.'

Parent of a 12 year-old boy

Under the UK Children's Acts and Order, disabled children and their families must be assessed and their needs addressed by social service or social work departments. This is particularly important for the children with complex additional needs in our survey. However, only just over half these children and young people had a social worker.

'I feel let down by social services. I receive no follow-up from my social worker, I have to constantly chase her. I receive no respite care whatsoever.'

Parent of a child with complex additional needs

Only one in two parents of children with a social worker felt their child's needs were being met by social work services. Half the parents would have liked more contact with social services or social work departments.

5.4 Breaks and respite

Most children enjoy breaks from their families from time to time, either with friends or relatives or in leisure activities. Many families welcome a regular break from caring for a disabled child, particularly if the child is severely disabled, but the opportunities are very limited. As part of their assessment of the child's and the family's needs, social service and social work departments should ensure there is adequate short break and respite care. Many of the parents in our study felt that there was inadequate provision for short breaks for carers.

'There is insufficient support for parents with children with a disability during the summer holidays, no holiday breaks for parents or carers.'

Parent of a six year-old girl

'I lost my respite overnight facility a year ago and pray it will be replaced. An active holiday is just a dream.'

Parent of a five year-old boy

For example:

- nearly six in ten families had no respite or short break care at all;
- only one in five families had access to free respite or short break services provided by social service or social work departments.

5.5 Inter-agency collaboration

'A more co-ordinated approach from professionals would make life a lot easier as case history would be followed up and acted upon, instead of repeated questions and methods.'

Parent of a 15 year-old boy

Children with complex needs may require support and care from many different service providers and agencies. Many parents in the focus groups expressed frustration at the perceived lack of joined-up working from the different care agencies. In the questionnaire survey only one in four parents thought that the different agencies helping their child worked well together.

'The various agencies have resources or access to specialist resources but they never seem to pool their advantages and knowledge. It is as though they are "serving" within a specific set limit rather than genuinely supporting an individual with difficulties throughout their stages of development.'

Parent of a 12 year-old boy

5.6 Equipment

Children and young people with complex additional needs frequently require specialist equipment for their day-to-day living. Some of this may be provided by the statutory services but much is not and parents often had difficulties in getting this equipment. In our survey:

- nearly four in ten parents of children with complex additional needs stated that they did not have items of equipment their children needed;
- the items most frequently named were computers, specially adapted chairs and associated structural changes to the house;
- two in three parents (65 per cent)

said their children did not have the equipment they needed because the family could not afford it.

5.7 Welfare benefits

It was evident from the research that clear, accessible information about benefits was crucial to receiving entitlements and that many parents were not receiving this. A significantly higher proportion of those who had received advice about benefits were receiving money than those who had not received advice.

- Nearly six in ten parents of children of around average learning ability had received no advice about benefits.
- One in five parents of children with complex additional needs had not received advice about benefits.
- Eight in ten older students who had not received benefits advice would have welcomed such information.

When asked questions about benefits, a number of the parents and most of the young people expressed reservations about discussing this topic. Some felt that it was a stigmatising issue:

'Being a carer and a mother is a full-time job, it's a shame people don't see it. To them we are spongers just receiving benefits. I think it's unfair.'
Parent of a 10 year-old girl

Others were strongly of the opinion that without the voluntary sector, the benefits system would be inadequate:

'Without the help of some charities my son would not have a bike to play on and be as normal as he can be.'
Parent of a seven year-old boy

Reference

Walker, E, Tobin, M and McKennell, A (1992). Blind and partially sighted children in Britain: the RNIB survey. HMSO, London.

Chapter 6

Study for a mural by **Tom Hunter** age
21, a partially sighted student at Queen
Alexandra College, Birmingham.

Shaping the future

The children, young people and parents who took part in the **Shaping the future** project did so on the understanding that their testimony would be used for the benefit of current and future generations of blind and partially sighted children and young people.

'I am pleased to help with this questionnaire as I believe it is important to let our thoughts be known, as it may help with future services.'
Parent of a nine year-old girl with complex additional needs

RNIB is committed to using the evidence in this summary report and the detailed research reports to help empower children, young people and their advocates; to raise awareness and reduce prejudice amongst the general public; to campaign for improved services and practice; and to identify areas for further research.

'A lot more research is needed to provide the visually impaired child with a rich, fulfilling, fun-filled childhood.'
Parent of a seven year-old boy

RNIB, the children, young people and parents involved in the project are keen to acknowledge the successes of the majority of blind and partially sighted children and young people in the UK today. But they also want to focus on the development of solutions to the problems and challenges faced by a significant number.

We believe that those solutions lie in fundamental changes in the attitudes of people who provide services, and of the general public, towards children and young people who are disabled. There also needs to be a change in emphasis in the planning and development of publicly available services. This requires:

- greater recognition of the potential and abilities of all blind and partially sighted children and young people;
- a greater voice for children, young people and their parents;
- increased support and resources

for inclusive education;

- increased access to inclusive mainstream facilities and activities;
- more opportunities to take part in specialised activities for those with similar abilities and experiences;
- appropriate, timely support for parents and families;
- greater collaboration between agencies working with and for blind and partially sighted children and young people and their families;
- young blind and partially sighted people and their advocates organising themselves.

6.1 Greater recognition of the potential and abilities of all blind and partially sighted children and young people

All children, whatever their abilities or impairments, have the potential to lead fulfilling, happy, successful lives but their opportunities can be severely limited if their strengths and aptitudes are not recognised. With appropriate support, blind and partially sighted children and young people can and do grow up to take as active a part in society as their sighted peers.

However, expectations can have an important effect on the development and success of children and young people and negative perceptions of disability can undermine the progress of those who are blind or partially sighted. Images of successful people with physical, sensory or learning impairments are unusual in today's media and in the public consciousness. Those with more severe impairments tend to be perceived as having little to offer a society dominated by economic and material values.

Our survey shows that a significant proportion of blind and partially sighted children and young people, both with and without complex additional needs, are aware of and affected by these unfounded prejudices. Recognising the ability and potential of each individual is one step on the road to dismantling the barriers faced by many blind and partially sighted children and young people in the UK today.

6.2 A greater voice for children, young people and their parents

The advantages of consultation for children, young people, their parents and for local service providers are enormous. Consultation can result in better service provision, better information, clients getting the services they need and want, and feelings of being valued and empowered. It also brings an understanding of the limitations and possibilities of service provision and better relationships between the people providing services and those using them.

Consulting blind and partially sighted children and young people and those with more complex needs must be done appropriately. The child's preferred means of communicating has to be considered. This means not just format, but also environment, timeframe, presence of others and so on. The child should have

control of this interaction as far as possible. If advocates or intervenors are involved they should know the child well and be fully conversant with the child's means of communication, needs and aspirations. As people better understand the communication needs and methods of children with complex additional needs, the more the children are able to learn to make choices and express their views, even if it is only on simple matters.

6.3 Increased support and resources for inclusive education

The responses of both parents and young people participating in this survey demonstrate that, whatever government policy may be, some people remain firm supporters of specialist education while others argue just as strongly in favour of full inclusion. Frequently, their opinions have been formed by very positive or very negative experiences of one or other type of provision.

'I would say the school he attends (mainstream) are very good at doing as much as they can to enable him to continue and have put in new lighting on the floors ... white treads on the stairs, repainted fences white etc ...'

Parent of a primary school boy

'I do not feel as though I was given enough help with choosing a school as I feel that he is in a school for physically handicapped children because the local authority want to keep as many children there as possible as numbers have fallen over the years. I feel as though he would have benefited socially from being in a mainstream school.'

Parent in a focus group

'I was worried about L going to school but he really enjoys it, and they involve him in everything. Even though he has numerous problems he has a happy, fulfilling life.'

Parent in a focus group

'Since attending the local secondary school, my son was singled out and bullied by a boy three school years higher than him ... Emotional damage has been caused ... For S, home education seems to be the only option.'

Parent of secondary pupil

Blind and partially sighted children and young people are individuals with unique needs that vary during the course of their development. RNIB therefore believes that a range of options should remain open to children and young people with visual impairments. This will allow parents, teachers and the young people themselves to choose the type of school that is most likely to meet the individual child's needs at the various stages of their school career.

Our findings point to a need for action in a number of areas:

• better awareness and training for teachers in mainstream schools about the needs of blind and partially sighted pupils, including specific information for subject teachers;
• improved communication between

teachers in schools about the requirements of their blind and partially sighted pupils;

- a discussion on the realistic resourcing of mainstream provision to ensure it provides the best possible support;
- increased awareness amongst providers of tertiary education about the support needs of blind and partially sighted students and the resource implications of inclusive provision;
- recognition in all areas of education that inclusive provision is as much about the ethos and social life of the school, college or university as it is about access to the curriculum.

6.4 Increased access to mainstream facilities and activities

Ensuring that blind and partially sighted children and young people have the same access to facilities and opportunities as their sighted peers requires that service planners and providers consider the needs of people with a range of physical, sensory and learning abilities at the outset. Adapting provision and activities that have been designed for sighted, non-disabled people is not always easy, can be expensive and may not result in successful inclusive provision. All sectors of statutory and voluntary services will be involved to some extent with blind and partially sighted children and young people and their planning should explicitly address such needs.

Planning inclusive provision and activities means considering: the individual needs of a wide range of people; environmental factors such as physical accessibility, lighting, signs, notices and auditory issues; accessible information; group dynamics; and staffing issues, including staff attitudes, numbers and expertise.

Information should be presented in formats that can be understood both by parents and children, including personal contact. The best way to provide this service and to comply with disability legislation is to have an accessible information policy that is internally enforceable.

Fully inclusive provision may have resource implications but will bring many long-term benefits for blind and partially sighted children and young people, their families and the whole community.

6.5 More opportunities to take part in specialised activities for those with similar abilities and experiences

As well as wanting greater access to mainstream provision, blind and partially sighted children, young people and their parents also want more opportunities to meet and socialise with others with similar experiences.

To develop their confidence, skills and independence, most blind and partially sighted children and young people benefit from receiving specialist support from those experienced in meeting their particular needs. This might include, for example mobility educators, specialists in communication skills, specialist teachers and experienced blind or partially sighted adults.

People from a particular group or community also gain strength and power from meeting others in similar circumstances. They are able to exchange experiences, compete on equal terms and develop a stronger identity. Opportunities for young blind and partially sighted people to meet with their peers are fundamental to the empowerment and development of these young people.

6.6 Appropriate, timely support for parents and families

The role of the parents and families of blind and partially sighted children must not be overlooked. The parents are sometimes the only advocates for the child's entitlement to good services:

'I have had to fight for most of the services and information I have needed to care for my son, I wish it were less of a struggle in the future for others.'
Parent at a focus group

Early, high quality support and information for parents at the time of diagnosis and at times of transition in their child's life are crucial to ensure that opportunities for social, emotional and educational development of the child and family are not restricted.

6.7 Greater collaboration between agencies

Successful inter-agency work is essential if services are to meet the needs of blind and partially sighted children and their families. At present this can be difficult because of different approaches between agencies; the time that professionals may need to meet and communicate; the fact that each service has its own dedicated budget; and difficulties that result from different statutory frameworks and boundaries.

In order to overcome the difficulties, agencies that work with blind and partially sighted children and young people should aim to ensure that:

- the rights and needs of the child are central to all planning;

- values are set out in joint statements;
- training is provided jointly and agencies share goals for services and performance;
- management teams co-operate;
- different teams exchange jobs and share experience;
- guidelines are clear about which agency or individual is taking the lead;
- budgets are managed jointly;
- programmes for monitoring and evaluation are jointly established and implemented.

6.8 Young people and their advocates organising themselves

The **Shaping the future** project involved a number of workshops and events that provided blind and partially sighted children with the opportunity to get together and share a vision. It became clear during these events how much young people wanted to be able to meet and campaign together. There is always a danger that organisations staffed by professionals take over and try

to run these activities for young
people or parents. Large
organisations of and for blind and
partially sighted people need to
support the endeavours of young
people and allow them to develop
and lead the campaigns for their
own rights.

At the last event a graffiti wall gave
them the opportunity to voice their
feelings.

Among the scribbles was this
rallying call from a young person:

'Stand up and be counted. Let the
world know we count, we matter
and we're tired of being shoved
aside.'

Suggested further reading

Anderson, P (1995). **Listening to children: children, ethics and social research.** Barnardos, Barkingside

Bentley, T and Oakley, K (1999). **The real deal: what young people really think about government, politics and social exclusion.** Demos, London

Clark, C, Dyson, A, Millward, A and Skidmore, D (1995). **Innovatory practice in mainstream schools for special educational needs.** HMSO, London

Department for Education and Employment (1998). **Meeting special educational needs: a programme of action.** DfEE, London

Department of Social Security (1999). **A new contract for welfare: children's rights and parents' responsibilities.** HMSO, London

Middleton, L (1999). **Disabled children: challenging social exclusion.** Blackwells, Oxford

Morris, J (1998). **Don't leave us out: involving disabled children and young people with communication impairments.** York Publishing Service/The Joseph Rowntree Foundation, York

Morris, J (1998). **Still missing: the experiences of disabled children and young people living away from their families.** The Who Cares? Trust, London

Shaw, C (1998). **Remember my messages: experiences and views of 2000 children in public care in the UK.** The Who Cares? Trust, London

Treseder, P (1997). **Empowering children and young people: training manual promoting involvement in decision making.** Children's Rights Office, Save the Children, London

Blind and partially sighted children and young people from schools and further education colleges in the following Education Authorities and Boards took part in the survey

Education Authorities

England

Barnsley
Bath and North East Somerset
Bedfordshire
Birmingham
Bromley
Buckinghamshire
Cornwall
Coventry
Doncaster
Dudley
East Sussex
Essex
Gloucestershire
Hampshire
Havering
Herefordshire
Hertfordshire
Hounslow
Kent
Kirklees
Lambeth
Lancashire
Leeds
Leicestershire
Liverpool
Manchester
Milton Keynes
Nene College
Newcastle
Newham
Northamptonshire
North Yorkshire
Northumberland
Nottinghamshire
Oldham
Redbridge
Salford
Sheffield
Shropshire
Somerset
South Tyneside
Staffordshire
Stockport
Suffolk
Surrey
Wandsworth
Westminster
Worcestershire
Wirral

Wales

Cardiff
Carmarthenshire
Flintshire
Gwynedd and Anglesey
Neath
Newport/Caerphilly
Rhondda
Swansea

Scotland

Dumfries and Galloway
Edinburgh
Falkirk
Fife
Glasgow
North Lanarkshire
Orkney
South Lanarkshire

Education Boards

Northern Ireland

Belfast
Southern
Western

Students from the following universities took part in the survey

England

East Anglia University
Greenwich University
John Moore's University, Liverpool
Leeds Metropolitan University
Manchester University
Nottingham Trent University
Reading University
Sheffield Hallam University
Staffordshire University
Sunderland University
Surrey University
Warwick University

Wales

Cardiff University
Swansea University

Scotland

Abertay University
Strathclyde University

RNIB services for children and young people

We run a wide range of services for children, young people, their families and the professionals who work with them. Our services aim to help children and young people to get the best possible start in life.

RNIB Education and Employment Information Service gives advice and support to parents, young people and professionals on everything from childcare to schooling to jobs. We support children, young people and adults in mainstream education. Our network of Education and Employment Centres provides training, specialised advice and support to families, professionals, blind and partially sighted students and those seeking work. RNIB Inclusive Education Services support the inclusion of blind and partially sighted children in mainstream schools and our Curriculum Information Service helps teachers to meet the needs of visually impaired pupils.

We run five schools for blind and partially sighted children and young people – four for those with additional complex needs and one secondary school for academically able pupils. Two colleges of further education offer a range of courses for school leavers and mature students.

Vacation Schemes give blind and partially sighted children in mainstream schools the chance to meet other visually impaired young people as well as try a range of exciting activities. Family Support Officers provide advice and support to families and run Family Weekends, enabling parents to meet others and talk to experts. Technology in Learning and Employment provides information on all aspects of technology, training for professionals, as well as assessment and training for pupils.

We also produce a range of publications and fact-sheets in a variety of media – braille, audio tape, large print and computer disk. For example, we transcribe exam papers into braille on behalf of schools and examination boards, and record children's books onto tape for our Talking Book Service. We also sell toys, puzzles and equipment for children and young people.

You can find out more by contacting us at the address below or visiting our website at www.rnib.org.uk There are special sections for parents (www.rnib.org.uk/parents) and students (www.rnib.org.uk/student).

RNIB Education and Employment Information Service
224 Great Portland Street, London W1N 6AA
Telephone: 020-7388 1266

RNIB Scotland Education Centre
Dunedin House, 25 Ravelston Terrace, Edinburgh EH4 3TP
Telephone: 0131-311 8500
Email: rnibscotland@rnib.org.uk

RNIB Northern Ireland Education Centre
21a Ormeau Avenue, Belfast BT2 8HD
Telephone: 028-9027 8118

RNIB Cymru Education Centre
Trident Court, East Moors Road, Cardiff CF24 5TD
Telephone: 029-204 50440